Albertine Gaur

Women in India

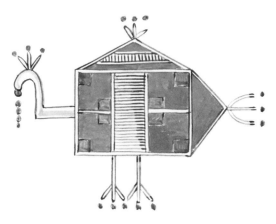

The British Library

British Library Booklets

It is the aim of this series of booklets to introduce the British Library to the general public by drawing attention to aspects of its collections which are of interest to the layman as well as the scholar. Many of the items mentioned and illustrated in the booklets are frequently on exhibition in the British Library's exhibition galleries in the British Museum building in Great Russell Street, London, W.C.1.

Acknowledgements

I would like to thank my colleagues Mr. J. Losty and Mr. M. I. Waley for checking the Sanskrit and Persian references, and Dr. Sayyid Darsh from the Islamic Cultural Centre in London for patiently answering questions on Islamic Law. The folk songs are part of a collection made by the late Dr. G. D. Gaur during the early part of 1950 for the purpose of a linguistic study. I would also like to thank Elaine Paintin for her critical comments.

© 1980 The British Library Board
Published by the British Library,
Great Russell Street, London, WC1B 3DG

🄱🄻 British Library Cataloguing in Publication Data
Gaur, Albertine
   Women in India.
   1. Women – India – Social conditions
   I. Title   II. British Library. *Reference Division.*
   301.41'2'0954   HQ1742

ISBN 0 904654 52 4
Designed by Peter Campbell
Set in Monophoto Ehrhardt
Printed in Great Britain by
Fletcher & Son Ltd, Norwich

Introduction

The position of women in Indian society has undergone several changes during the 4000 years which make up the history of the subcontinent. Apart from conquests and population movements which introduced new concepts the caste, class, economic status, geographical region and religious affinity of the family to which a woman belongs have always greatly influenced her standing within the community. Hinduism and Islam, the two major religions of India, have basically different attitudes towards women. Each attitude has become enshrined in traditional laws, in the case of Islam by the Qur'ān (7th cent. AD) in the case of Hinduism by Manu and other Brahmanical law givers (500 BC–AD 500). Both brought about changes in the position of women, but whereas the Qur'ān introduced a more liberal attitude, Manu severely curtailed the social and sexual freedom and the ritual importance Hindu women had enjoyed in earlier periods.

Law and tradition are moreover open to interpretation as they always have been. They can be applied in a liberal way with the stress on benefits or in an exploitative way with the stress on repression. From the purely legal standpoint the Muslim woman seems to fare better as she can own and dispose of property, conduct business and remarry if her husband dies or divorces her. Against this must be set that she is expected to veil herself in front of all men and live in the strict seclusion of the women's quarter, if the family is rich enough to afford such luxuries. The Hindu woman on the other hand is considered a potential source of power which, if not properly controlled, can bring danger and ritual pollution to her family and society as a whole. Manu insists (and Schopenhauer would probably have agreed with him) that a woman must at all times be kept under the supervision of a man: in childhood of her father, in youth of her husband and in old age of her son. Though widows are of course no longer burned, and unwanted female children are no longer disposed of, it is still rare for a Hindu to marry a woman who has already lived with another husband and in the majority of families boys will get more attention in matters of care, diet and education. But since the laws of Manu did not derive from divine revelation Hinduism is more receptive to reform than Islam which must not deviate from the word of the Prophet.

Islam was established in India only in the 12th century AD and like most cultures transplanted to an alien environment lost much of its original strength and purity. Veiling, for example, which had originally only meant covering all parts of the body save the hands and the face was extended to wearing the all enveloping black *burqa*, and the Hindu acceptance of prostitution had some influence on the attitude of at least the wealthy classes. Religious minority groups such as Jews, Christians and Parsis, and certain tribes, have always made an attempt to conform to the Hindu idea of respectability; in fact if a particular group wishes to raise its social status it usually prohibits the eating of meat, and the re-marriage of widows. During the last two centuries laws have been passed which have greatly improved and reformed the position of women but it must be remembered that even today nearly 80% of Indians live in rural areas where the approval of the family, the caste and the rest of the village community are more important and offer greater protection than legislation passed in Delhi (or Calcutta).

It would be folly to attempt a full account of the history and position of Indian women in so short a space. India is a plural society *par excellence*. It is possible to illustrate quite contradictory attitudes, all of which would contain an element of truth and this paradox is one of the great charms of Indian life and the great strength of Indian society. In all this plurality there are however basic concepts of femaleness which colour the attitude of society and the expectations of the woman herself. All that the present publication attempts is to show visually, with the aid of illustrations from manuscripts in the British

3

Library, a few of these concepts, examine them, place them side by side and leave it to the reader to assemble them into a picture. This picture will by necessity be subjective and incomplete but it may at least create curiosity and a desire to know more.

Or. 11387. f. 80 (a)

A metrical version (in Assamese) of the *Brahmakhāṇḍa* of the *Brahmavaivarta purāṇa* by Durgācārya. AD 1836/7.

Nūr Jahān

1974.6.17.010. (23).

British Museum, Department of Oriental Antiquities.
Nūr Jahān with attendants on a terrace. Provincial Mughal; Oudh. 18th century.

Or. 2976. f. 74 (b)

The *Bahmanāma* by Īrānshāh ibn Abī'l-Khair; AD 1836. Bhaman playing polo with his future wife Humāy, daughter of the King of Egypt.

Nūr Jahān, or as she was originally called Mihr an-Nisā, was the daughter of a Persian official at the court of the Mughal Emperor Akbar (AD 1556–1605). At seventeen she was married to 'Alī Qulī, a Persian adventurer who received several titles on the accession of Akbar's son Jahāngīr (AD 1605–1627). After the death of her husband she was brought to the imperial harem in Delhi where she became an attendant of Akbar's widow Sālima.

1974. 6.17.010. (23)

Unlike Hinduism Islam attaches no stigma to widowhood, in fact Khadija, the first wife of the Prophet was the widow of a prosperous merchant and Muḥammad was in her service before he married her. (She was also considerably older than he).

In 1611 Jahāngīr, attracted by Mihr an-Nisā's exquisite beauty married her and changed her name to Nūr Jahān (Light of the World). The chronicles credit her with many outstanding qualities: beauty, intellect, a love for poetry and an exceedingly shrewd political judgement. Like other noble Muslim ladies (see Or. 2976) she was skilled in the royal sports and in 1619 she killed a tiger with one shot. Nūr Jahān had great influence over her husband who left her more or less entirely in charge of the administration. According to popular stories she was often present at public audiences where, hidden behind a curtain, she would supply her husband with suitable answers whenever he faltered.

A Royal Muslim Wife

1920.9.17.0206

British Museum, Department of Oriental Antiquities.

Portrait of Mumtāz Mahal. Probably 18th century.

Mumtāz Mahal, a niece of Nūr Jahān, was given in marriage to Jahāngīr's favourite son Khurram, later the Muslim Emperor Shāh Jahān (AD 1628–1658). Though she did not possess her aunt's political brilliance she inspired great devotion in her husband who, when she died at the age of 39 at the birth of their 14th child, built the fabled Taj Mahal as her tomb. Shāh Jahān's devotion did not end with Mumtāz Mahal's death. His original plan had been to build a mausoleum for himself on the other side of the river Jamuna but prolonged and bitter family feuds intervened. Eventually his son Aurangzeb (AD 1658–1680) imprisoned him in the Red Fort of Agra and Shāh Jahān spent the last years of his life – according to his own wish – in a room from where he could at least see the Taj Mahal.

Hinduism and Islam both glorify motherhood. But there is little room for romantic attachment between husband and wife within the closely-knit hierarchical structure of a Hindu joint family. Since all members (i.e. the parents with their sons and the sons'

wives) live under one roof, eat food cooked in the same kitchen and jointly own all property a husband who becomes infatuated with his wife is a potential source of danger to the unity and welfare of the whole family. He may side with her in quarrels, make special provision for her and her children, or – the ultimate fear – demand his share of the property to set up an independent household. The newly-wedded wife is therefore watched with a certain amount of apprehension by the rest of the family.

My mother-in-law speaks to me
only in anger
my eldest sister-in-law
who knows many heart-piercing words
rebukes me at every occasion.
What can I tell you about the rest?
The mere thought of them makes me shiver.
Oh Sakhi (girl-friend), I have but one fault
my husband looks at me with affection.

(Translation of an unpublished Hindi folk-song from northern India.)

Parsi Women

1974.6.17.01. f. 17.
British Museum, Department of Oriental Antiquities.
Drawing of a Zoroastrian woman from an album of costumes, animals and maps, mostly prepared in Isfahan in AD 1684–5.

The Zoroastrians, or Parsis as they are generally called, are descendants of Persian immigrants who came to India in the 8th century AD when their country was conquered by the Arabs. The principles of their religion are based on the teachings of Zoroaster (*ca.* 1200–700 BC). They worship fire, expose their dead, and adhere to certain principles of ritual purity. Parsi women enjoy a reasonable amount of freedom and equality. Girls as well as boys are instructed in the religious texts and both wear the ritual garment, the sacred shirt (sadra) and the girdle (kusti) given to them at initiation. Parsi women are allowed to worship in the fire temple though certain restrictions apply during menstruation which is considered a period of ritual impurity. Like other Indian communities the Parsis do not approve of mixed marriages but a non-Parsi woman married to a Parsi is accepted to the extent that her children are considered Parsis. If, however, a Parsi girl marries outside her group she will be excommunicated and her children can never be Parsis. Until the early 19th century Parsi women kept their traditional place in the home where they played a major part in the domestic rituals: tending the hearth fire, censing the house with brazier and incense at sunset, doing the ritual cooking in strict purity and training the children in their religious duties. In the latter part of the century, after reformers had founded girls' schools, women began to take a more active part in public life, even attending the *gahambar* feasts which had, up to then, been an all male preserve. Education and material prosperity have eroded some of the traditional values and in most urban homes, electricity, gas or oil have replaced the hearth fire and thus eliminated the centre of family devotion. Modern Parsi girls, especially from the prosperous urban merchant classes, are usually well educated and – as far as this is possible within the context of Indian society – fairly independant. The traditional costume (see illustration) has more or less disappeared. Like the majority of Jewish and Christian women in India, Parsi girls now wear the sari.

8

ردس شوقضننا كهرام آغا

Courtesans

Or. 8838. ff. 10, 12.

An album of *rāgas and rāgiṇīs* (visual representations of musical modes) with descriptive verses in Hindi. 19th century.

f. 10.   A courtesan at her toilette attended by the old woman who was essential to the courtesan as maid, confidante and go-between.

Or. 8838. f. 12

f. 12. The maid has brought a client (a prospective lover or a lover who has been in disgrace) who prostrates himself at the courtesan's feet in an attempt to win her favour.

A substantial part of Hindu literature describes the beauty, functions and accomplishments of courtesans and prostitutes, the science of sexual technique, the definition of (erotic) emotions and their relation to music, painting, literature, particular types of landscape and certain times of the day and the year. Sanskrit, the classical language of

11

India, has innumerable synonyms for the word prostitute, indicating the strict hierarchy of this profession. No stigma was attached to the *devadāsīs*, the temple women, who were dedicated to the service of the deity in the temple, often by their own parents (to win religious merit, to ensure the birth of a son, in fulfilment of a vow etc.). Their training in dancing and in the erotic arts started at around the age of seven and, later, after a formal marriage ceremony when the *tāli* was tied round their necks, they were ritually de-flowered either by a Brahmin priest, a privileged patron of the temple or by being made to sit astride a stone *liṅgam* (phallus). At weddings their presence was considered aus-picious as, being married to the god, they could never become widows. The great temples of Tanjore, Madurai, Kanchipuram and Somnath had hundreds of *devadāsīs* in their service but by the beginning of the 20th century Christian missionaries and Hindu reformers had more or less succeeded in eliminating the profession.

The *Arthaśāstra*, the classical text of Hindu statecraft (*ca*. 300 BC) mentions the state prostitute who served as a spy and intelligence agent, and whose earnings supplied much needed revenues. In the Vijayanagar Empire (AD 1336–1642) the entire police force of 12,000 men is said to have been, at one time, financed in this way. High-ranking too was the *rāja kanyā*, the King's girl (not necessarily his mistress), who was present at certain state functions when she stood behind the throne holding the royal umbrella. The *gaṇikās* were in most cases accomplished singers and dancers and the only women who enjoyed the privilege of being taught how to read. They were usually one man's mistress or selected their clients from among a few men of the rich and noble classes. The *bayadère* and *nautch* girls of European travellers' tales came mostly from this class. Lowest on the scale, and the only one who survived the decline of the rich Hindu kingdoms and the zeal of 19th-century reformers, is the *veśyā*, the common harlot. Once recruited from the ranks of discarded courtesans, widows and barren wives, they now also include the very poor or unfortunate young girls who have fallen foul of the Hindu code of morality which makes virginity an essential prerequisite for marriage. (They also include some European women.)

Many texts deal with the science of sexual technique and emotion (*kāmaśāstra*), the first, with 100,000 chapters, being ascribed to the god Prajāpati. The best known work, the *Kāmasutra*, is supposed to have been written by *Vātsyāyana* (*ca*. AD 200) who according to tradition was an ascetic and celebate. A quite different person was Kokkoka (*ca*. 11th/12th century AD), another exponent of the *kāmaśāstra* about whom it is told that once an amorous *yakṣī* (celestial nymph) came to the court of his patron and com-plained that in all the fourteen worlds she had visited, neither gods, demons nor men had been able to satisfy her. Kokkoka remedied this problem with such skill that she lost all erotic desire for the next seven incarnations.

The Muslim Family

O4. 12988. f. 114 (a) (Colour, p. 13)

Akbarnāma by Abu' l-Faẓl ibn Mubārak. Mughal. AD 1603/4. The Mughal Emperor Humāyūn (d. AD 1556) at the celebration held at the circumcision of his son Akbar. The infant Akbar is held by his mother Maryam Makānī and the royal couple are attended by Zenana women and entertained by dancing girls. Outside the walls of the women's quarters the Emperor's subjects join the festivities.

A Muslim marriage is a legally binding contract which places certain well-defined obli-gations on both parties. The contract itself is concluded between the bridegroom and the bride's guardian (usually the nearest male relation) and normally the bride's consent is required. A vital part is the *mahr* which the husband has to give to the wife in exchange

12

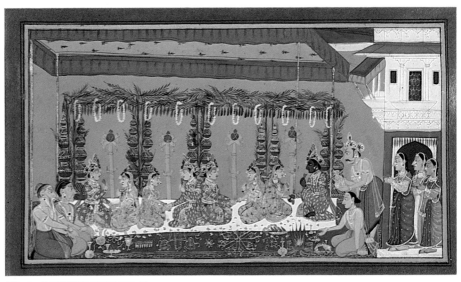

Add. 15295. f. 199(a) (Hindu marriage, see p. 17)

for the absolute right he acquires over her; the form and amount of the *mahr* differs according to the tradition of the community to which the couple belong. To make the marriage valid at least two (male) witnesses are required. The ceremony itself is simple (not day-long feasts as with Hindus) and does not require the presence of a religious functionary. Whatever property the woman owns at the time of marriage remains her own and, in addition, the husband is expected to support her in the style to which she has so far been accustomed; if he cannot fulfil this obligation, or if he is unable to provide the *mahr* the woman can ask for the dissolution of marriage. (She can also ask for the dissolution of marriage if the husband takes a further wife without her consent or if she has truly lost all love for him.) In return the wife has to be obedient, faithful, chaste, mindful of the rules of proper conduct laid down by the Qur'ān for Muslim women and ready for intercourse; if she is found wanting she can be chastised and/or divorced. A Muslim is allowed to have four wives whom he must, however, treat in exactly the same way as far as financial support and sexual attention is concerned. Children are legitimate if they are born at least six months after consummation and not more than four years after divorce or dissolution. The adoption of children is forbidden since this would lead to conflicts with the laws governing inheritance and prohibited marriage partners. A Muslim family can however extend 'love, care and guardianship' to a child without severing him from his natural family. Though children are one of the main purposes of marriage, birth-control by *coitus interruptus* is permitted (with the consent of the wife) for economic reasons and to safeguard the health (and beauty) of the woman. Divorce is the sole right of the husband but such a step is neither encouraged nor should it be undertaken lightly. It is, in fact, thought to be the most hated thing in the sight of God. Only after attempts at reconciliation and arbitration between the couple themselves and representatives of their families have failed may the husband exercise his right and pronounce *ṭalāq*. This step obliges him to hand over the rest of the *mahr* (half if the marriage has not been consummated) after the period of waiting ('*idda*) has passed. '*Idda*, which lasts normally between three to four months, is to ensure that the wife is not pregnant. If she is pregnant her '*idda* ends on the day of delivery. During this period the husband is obliged to house and maintain the woman. He is also free to take her back if he chooses. Once '*idda* is over the woman can remarry; the same applies in the case of a widow.

Or. 2265. f. 157(b) (Scenes from a Romantic Poem, see p. 18)

Hindu Marriage

Add. 15295. f. 199 (a) (Colour, p. 14)
Vālmīki's *Rāmāyaṇa*; Sanskrit text. AD 1713. Three couples being married.

Marriage is one of the major sacraments (*samskāras*) for Hindus and the only one which is open to women and low caste people. Though eight different forms of marriage were traditionally recognised, most of them are no longer in use and some were indeed little more than sanctification of rape (*paiśāca*), kidnapping (*rākṣasa*) or ritual intercourse (*śaiva/cakrapūja*). Extinct too is *svayamvara*, a variation of the *gāndharva* type of marriage, i.e. 'the marriage between a desiring woman with a desiring man' which, though idealised in classical literature was not encouraged in practice. The basis of a regular Hindu marriage is *brāhmya* where the partners are selected by the parents, the bride is provided with a dowry and, in the course of a religious ceremony conducted by a Brahmin priest, is given 'properly bedecked and ornamented' as a gift to the bridegroom. The actual marriage rites may vary according to caste, sectarian belief and local custom but there are certain obligatory rituals, the most crucial one being *agni-pradakṣiṇa*, during which the bride and the bridegroom walk round the sacred fire. During the *homa* sacrifice when clarified butter is poured into the flame the bridegroom, holding the bride's hand, utters the words: 'Oh my bride, be thou pleasant to the members of my family and to the cattle we possess; give birth to heroic children; never miscarry and never have an empty lap.'

Marriage is not a personal matter but a family affair. It is the duty of the girl's father to search for a bridegroom as soon as she has reached puberty. Indeed the Brahmanical lawgivers condemn to hell a father in whose house a daughter 'wastes' her first menstruation – a dictum which greatly encouraged child-marriage. In the often delicate negotiations between the two families the girl's family is at a definite disadvantage and conditions are usually laid down by the other side. Once the girl is married she goes to her father-in-law's house where she will be under the strict supervision of her husband's mother. Her own family is not encouraged to visit her, 'one does not eat one's own dowry' is a saying commonly used in the villages. Folksongs often describe the thoughts and worries of the girl who is the subject of the transaction.

Send for five betel leaves, O my father
and for five roots of tumeric
have green and tender bamboo cut, O my father
and build a pavilion in the orchard
where our fathers can sit and gamble.
Who is the winner, who is the loser
and what is the price?
Father is the loser, father-in-law the winner
and the bride is the price.
My father was the loser
the day I was born
my father-in-law was the winner
the day my bridegroom was born.

(Translation of an unpublished folksong from Northern India.)

The Goddess in Hinduism

Stowe Or. 22. (Colour, p. 15)

Devī māhātmya (left column) and *Bhagavad gītā* (right column), two Sanskrit poems. 18/19th century. The illustrations which are at the beginning of the manuscript show, on the left: Gaṇeśa, Sarasvatī, Gaga Lakṣmī, Kālī, Durgā, and on the right: Gaṇeśa, Sarasvatī and Brahmā, Lakṣmī and Viṣṇu, Pārvatī and Śiva, and finally Kṛṣṇa and Arjuna.

The deeply-rooted ambivalence towards the female as both a nurturing and a destructive figure is reflected in the various forms of the goddess in the Hindu pantheon. Benevolent goddesses are those who have transferred control of their sexuality (power-*śakti*, nature-*prākṛti*) to their husbands. It is this transfer which makes gods divine and protects men from misfortune and even death. Married, the goddess is always good. Unmarried, she can be good or bad. She can be good if she herself has achieved control of her power, either through extreme austerities or (particularly sexual) abstinence. But if she has failed to do so she remains nature (*prākṛti*) and pure nature is always unpredictable and dangerous. Thus Durgā, one of the terrible goddesses, rides on a tiger (or lion) and is accompanied by eight demonesses who complete her work of destruction by chewing the bones left over from her gory repasts. Kālī, the 'black one' who brings pestilence, death and terror was patron goddess of the Thugs, a fraternity of assassins who strangled their victims in her honour. They were not supposed to harm women but they themselves attributed their downfall (the British administration succeeded in eliminating them between 1830 and 1860) to the fact that some of their members had angered the goddess by offering her female victims.

Scenes from a Romantic Poem

Or. 2265. f. 157 (b) (Colour, p. 16)

Khamsa, a romantic Persian poem by Nizāmī (born AD 1141); Safavid/Tabriz. AD 1539–43.

The miniature shows Majnūn being brought in chains by the old woman to Layla's tent. The other women in the camp are seen attending to their customary tasks such as cooking, milking, embroidering, washing clothes and looking after children.

The *Khamsa* relates the story of Layla and Qays, the children of two tribal chieftains who grew up together in Baghdad. When Layla's people leave the city for the hills Qays becomes Majnūn (mad). Though his father follows the tribe in an attempt to arrange a marriage, Majnūn's madness does not recommend him as a prospective son-in-law and Layla is married to the rich Ibn Salām instead. After her husband's death Layla sends for Majnūn hoping that now, at last, they can be united but Majnūn is no longer able to adjust to reality, his sorrow and grief for her initial loss have turned him into an ascetic and he flees her presence.

Muslim romantic poetry, based mostly on Persian prototypes, abounds in stories of the mad, heart-broken lover. The Hindu prototype of the romantic lover is the god Kṛṣṇa whose charm seduces the *gopīs* (milk maids) who forget their husbands and children and go in search of him when they hear his flute in the middle of the night. His favourite among them, Rādhā, is the subject of innumerable miniature paintings where she is shown braving darkness, lightning, snakes and other perils of the forest on her way to their clandestine meeting place, or waiting there patiently amidst fading garlands she has prepared in his honour – Kṛṣṇa usually being late or not coming at all. In Hindu literature it is nearly always the woman who waits, laments and at times destroys herself. Folksongs too favour this motive though, in these, the lovers are usually married – illicit love being more acceptable in mythology and art – and the husband has gone to the nearby town in search of work. His absence means that his wife is excluded from the seasonal festivities in the village and, as time goes by, her fear of having been permanently abandoned increases.

O Sakhi [girl-friend], *Sāvan* has come,
all are dyeing the hemp
and getting the ropes made
only I am fading away.
Oh Sakhi, *Bhadon* has come,
lightning flashes and frightens me
the nights are very dark
only I am fading away.
Oh Sakhi, *Kvar* has come,
all draw auspicious patterns
and wear the red mark on their forehead
only I am fading away.
Oh Sakhi, *Kārtik* has come,
all the lamps are burning
everybody bathes in holy water
only I am fading away.
Oh Sakhi, *Aghan* has come,
all are getting new garlands made
and have the parting of their hair coloured
only I am fading away.
Oh Sakhi, *Pus* has come,
all are having their quilts filled
and prepare comfortable beds
only I am fading away.
Oh Sakhi, *Māgh* has come,
all are happy by the warm fire
and bath in hot water
only I am fading away.
Oh Sakhi, *Phāgun* has come,
all prepare coloured water
all celebrate Holi
only I am fading away.
Oh Sakhi, *Cait* has come,
all peep through the windows
and enjoy the moonlit nights
only I am fading away.
Oh Sakhi, *Baisakh* has come,
all rest by the fan
all have their saris dyed
only I am fading away.
Oh Sakhi, *Jeth* has come,
in the forest the buds are fading

they are all getting their houses thatched with grass
only I am fading away.
Oh Sakhi, *Āsādh* has come,
all quench the fire of their hearts
in the forest shriek the peacocks
only I am fading away.
Mother, you have come in time
the fire has not yet touched my hair
without my husband I may as well be *sati*.

(Translation of an unpublished Hindi folk-song from northern India. *Sāvan, Bhadon,*
etc. are local names of the Hindu lunar months.)

Add. 5638. f. 233(a)

The Attempted Rape of Draupadī

Add. 5638. f. 233 (a)

Persian version of the *Mahābhārata*, translated by Naķīb Khān and others. Written in Muradabad. Provincial Mughal. AD 1761–3.

The *Mahābhārata* tells, with innumerable interpolations, the story of the great war between the Kauravas and the Pāṇḍavas, two rival factions of one royal family. The five Pāṇḍava brothers, who throughout the story are portrayed as the 'good' heroes, were conceived according to the Hindu custom of *niyoga* which, under certain circumstances allowed a childless woman to employ an 'indrenching agent' in the form of a brother-in-law (if she was a widow), a Brahmin or, as in the legendary case of the two mothers of the Pāṇḍavas whose common husband Pāṇḍu had been unable to consummate the marriage because of a curse, a god. Children born of such a union were considered legitimate issues of the woman's husband; thus the name Pāṇḍavas. At one point in the story the Pāṇḍavas learned that the King of Panchāla had proclaimed a *svayamvara* at which his daughter Draupadī was to select a husband from among the suitors. Disguised as Brahmins the Pāṇḍavas attended the *svayamvara* and Arjuna, a mighty bowman and warrior defeated everybody, including the hundred Kaurava brothers who were among the competitors. On their return home Arjuna's mother, when told that he had won a great treasure, unwittingly advised him to share it with his brothers. Thus Draupadī became the common wife of all the five Pāṇḍava brothers and to avoid jealousy it was decided that she should dwell for two days with each of them in turn.

The illustration on the cover of the booklet depicts one of the key episodes of the *Mahābhārata*: the gambling match between Yudhiṣṭhira, the eldest Pāṇḍava brother and Śakuni, an uncle of the Kaurava princes, a great gambler and cheat. In the course of the dice game Yudhiṣṭhira loses everything, his wealth, his palaces, his kingdom, his four brothers, himself and finally Draupadī. Duryodhana, the dominant Kaurava brother, has Draupadī dragged into the assembly and Duḥśāsana, the most wicked of the brothers, proceeds to tear off her clothes. Draupadī implores the help of the god Kṛṣṇa who miraculously increases the length of her sari so that a new layer of material appears everytime Duḥśāsana has removed one.

Jewish, Christian and Anglo-Indian Women

1974. f. 76.

Galsulkar (Hayyim Isaac)'s Marathi translation of the *Haggādāh*. Jewish women preparing bread for the Sabbath. Poona 1874.

Jewish and Christian communities have existed in India since the early centuries of the Christian era. Both favour female education and indeed did so long before Hindus found the idea acceptable. The Hindu caste system has made some inroads and there are prohibitions in regard to inter-marriage between certain sub-groups of each community. Nowadays most women wear the sari except for some of the St. Thomas (Syrian) Christians in Kerala (southwest of India) who use a cloth of sari length but arrange it in fan-like pleats at the back, and an upper garment which, unlike the sari blouse, always covers the arms and midriff. When going to church they will wrap themselves from head to foot in a white shawl which leaves only the face free. Like most South Indian women

1974. f. 76

they have the *tāli* (a type of necklace) tied round their neck at the time of marriage, but their *tāli* is tied by the priest in church and has a cross as pendant. Apart from ordinary earrings they wear a special type of heavy golden ornament in the upper lobe of the ear.

Most Christian girls have jobs, not only as teachers (the most acceptable profession), lawyers, doctors or politicians (only possible for a very small number of privileged upper class women) but, like Anglo-Indian girls, they will also work as nurses, a profession most Hindus find abhorrent since it offends against the ideas of status (rendering personal service to somebody outside the immediate family), caste (coming into close contact with somebody from another caste) and propriety (coming into close physical contact with men).

The position of Anglo-Indian girls is an uneasy one. Mostly educated in Christian schools, dressed like Europeans and allowed a similar amount of social freedom they are constantly suspected of immorality by most Hindu men. Hindu families will rather accept a Western daughter-in-law (painful as this may be) than an Anglo-Indian girl. The problem is poignantly illustrated in Satjit Ray's film *Maha Nagar* (Big City) by the pretty Anglo-Indian sales girl who immediately loses her job when she falls ill because her boss refuses to believe in her illness; as far as he is concerned she has only stayed away from work because she wanted 'to be with men'.

Sītā's Ordeal

Add. 5638. f. 363 (b)
Persian version of the *Mahābhārata*. AD 1761–3.

Sītā's fire ordeal as described in the *Rāmāyaṇa*.

The *Rāmāyaṇa* (in one version already incorporated in the *Mahābhārata*) relates the story of Rāma, the eldest son of the King of Ayodhyā. An envious stepmother, who covets the throne for her own son, causes him to spend fourteen years as an exile in the forest accompanied only by his loyal brother Lakṣmaṇa and his devoted wife Sītā who was married to him when she was six years of age. During this period Sītā is kidnapped by Rāvaṇa, the demonic king of Sri Lanka. With the help of allies Rāma eventually defeats Rāvaṇa and rescues Sītā. Though Sītā has remained faithful to Rāma throughout her long captivity, Rāma does not accept her back before she has proved her chastity through a fire ordeal. Sītā, ever obedient to her husband, enters the fire 'in the presence of gods and men' and Agni, the god of fire himself, returns her, unharmed, to Rāma. Rāma is crowned and embarks on a glorious reign with Sītā as his Queen. Yet after some time a washerman in the city whose wife had been absent from home for one night refuses to take her back, saying, he was not like the King who took his wife back after she had spent years in another man's house. With this the gossip starts and though the gods themselves have vouched for Sītā's honour and she is then carrying Rāma's child, he banishes her to the forest. The story of Sītā and Rāma enjoys enormous popularity all over India: Rāma is considered the ideal man, Sītā the ideal wife. This obsession with female chastity which condemns a woman even on the basis of the most unfounded gossip permeates the whole concept of Hindu marriage and Hindu life. It is the wife's chastity which protects the husband and even today there are fishermen in southern India who will refuse to share a man's boat if his wife has been the object of rumour, fearing the sea will take them all if only one of them has lost the protective shield of his wife's self-sacrificing devotion. Islam too greatly prizes chastity and considers the death sentence a fit punishment for the adulterous wife. But anybody who accuses a woman of adultery without being able to prove his accusation, the only acceptable proof being the confession of the woman or four witnesses to the moment of penetration, can be sentenced to 80 lashes and his testimony will never again be considered trustworthy.

Add. 5638. 1. 363(b)

Daily Life of Hindu Women

Or. 11689. (4 folios)

Bhāgavata purāṇa; Sanskrit text in Oriya script. Orissa. 18th century.

Or. 11612. (4 folios)

Rādhākṛṣṇa keli kathā; Oriya poem on Kṛṣṇa's life in Brindaban. Orissa. 17th century.

If the wedding ceremony is the only ritual in which a Hindu woman can participate, marriage is the sole justification for her existence, her husband the only god she may

worship. Being born a woman is considered the penalty for sins committed in a previous existence and the only possible salvation lies in being *pativratā* (husband-devoted) and *patidevatā* (husband-worshipping). This complete devotion is obligatory irrespective of the husband's moral value; as the *Padma purāṇa* puts it: 'be a husband aged, infirm, deformed, debauched, offensive, a drunkard, a gambler, a frequenter of places of ill repute, living in open sin with other women and destitute of honour, still a wife should regard him as a god.'

The illustrations, taken from two palm-leaf manuscripts, give an account of the services a good wife is expected to render: milking the cows, cooking, serving food to the husband (she is not supposed to eat with him, or worse, before him), tending the children, giving her breast to an infant (male), nursing him to sleep on her lap. After the husband has eaten he stretches out on his bed and she massages his feet. Only when he is comfortable may she eat what is left over and another, older child (female) comes and is given the rest of the food. Finally she prepares herself for joining him on the bed to provide *rati* (sexual pleasure) for the purpose of conceiving (it is hoped) male offspring who will perpetuate the family and perform the all-important funeral rites for their dead father.

Wall Paintings by Indian Women

These designs are copies of small wall paintings which the village women around Jaipur (Rajasthan) draw on both sides of the entrance at the time of weddings and childbirth, especially at the birth of a son. If a girl is born in the area people inquiring may be told that 'nothing' has been born. The collection was made in 1962/3 by the author and altogether 22 designs were copied. Size and position was usually the same, outlines were always drawn in brown, the colours used were red, yellow, blue and green. Motives varied, most were clearly traditional (the tree of life, the pitcher, the fan, the lamp, peacocks, dancers), others were highly stylised and in some cases modern observation seems to have intruded (there was one locomotive).

The drawing of auspicious patterns and designs is throughout India a task traditionally assigned to women. More prevalent and more universally used than the above colourful wall paintings are *raṅgolis*, patterns of pure design mostly in one colour (white),

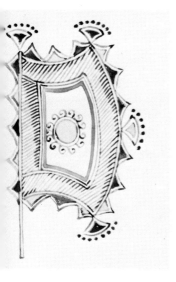

which are used to decorate thresholds, courtyards, ceremonial platforms, the floors of living areas or, in bigger establishments, at least the floor of the *pūja* room; i.e. the room used for worship. Elaborate *rangolis* are drawn at festive occasions, such as wedding ceremonies (see Add. 15295), more simple ones will be fashioned by female members of the family – or perhaps a female servant – every morning outside the family home, not only in the rural areas but also among more traditional groups living in big cities such as Madras, Bangalore or Delhi. The technique consists either of sprinkling rice powder between thumb and fingers on the ground or of wrapping a piece of cloth soaked in a thin mixture of rice powder and water round one finger; in the case of especially large designs the cloth is wrapped round a wooden stick. The tradition itself may go back as far as the Indus Valley culture (*ca.* 2500 BC). In historical times *rangolis* have generally been considered auspicious areas for welcoming deities. Patterns of this kind, referred to as *maṇḍalas*, are mentioned in Buddhist and Hindu philosophy where they are used as focal points for meditation, and in Tantric cults where they are thought to represent the female organ.

Women and Slavery

Or. 8758. f. 54 (a)

Qiṣṣad-i Sayf al-Mulūk va Badī' al-Jamāl. Copied by Muḥammad Wārith. Thatta AD 1755.

Tāj al-Mulūk bestowing slave girls on Sayf al-Mulūk watched by Sa'īd.

Though Islam did not abolish slavery it ameliorated some of the moral and legal aspects of the institution. It forbade the use of female slaves for prostitution and ruled that nobody must enjoy them except their legal masters. A man was allowed sexual intercourse with his own slaves but not with a slave belonging to his wife – even with the wife's consent; indulgence was however shown in relation to slaves belonging to a son. Children born to a slave woman could not be separated from their mother before they had reached the age of seven (this still applies to divorced women) and their birth greatly enhanced the mother's position. She could no longer be sold and was usually given her freedom at the death of the child's father. A man could marry a Christian or Jewish slave girl (though not a heathen) who did not have to change her religion and became emancipated upon marriage. According to the Qur'ān freeing a slave falls into the same category as giving alms and a two-fold reward was promised to the man who educated his slave girl and married her.

Indian Women Today

The vast majority of Indian women live in villages, adhering to traditional values, carrying out traditional tasks, most of them barely aware of the laws which have been passed for their benefit. Literacy rates are low, a mere 20% of the total female population. Even in urban areas only economically and socially advanced families can provide their daughters with what is still referred to as a 'Western' education. The fact that it is mainly this group which can afford to travel abroad and meet visitors, which attracts the attention of the media, has at times created the impression that the educated Indian woman of today is 'modern' in a Western sense.

But being taught a similar set of intellectual skills – and unlike education in the home which stresses values, formal education in India concentrates mainly on the acquisition

خوب رویی و ساقیان ماه یار انجمن را تازه تر دا شتند

of skills – does not turn an Indian woman into a Western woman. Her life is spent in a society where status and formal obligations outweigh personal relationships, where both men and women are taught that submission of the individual to family and society and deliberate self control over spontaneous impulses are the characteristics of civilised people. A handful of women in Parliament, in the Law Courts and in possession of University chairs does not mean change: they are simply the exception. Change would mean large numbers of women working as waitresses, nurses, in shops, factories and offices. The objective of the training and education of an Indian girl is still marriage and the highest status an Indian woman can obtain is still motherhood, preferably of a son. Spinsters are rare and viewed with a certain amount of mistrust as are widows, foreign wives and prostitutes. Most marriages are arranged and free mixing of the sexes is not encouraged.

Even professional women will in most cases place the interests of their families (husbands, fathers and sons) before their careers. Little girls are still told by fond relatives 'you will be another Sita'. Women are viewed with a mixture of desire and hostility, hardly surprising in a society based on caste and group responsibility where an erring member can harm the whole community. On this point village and town agree. As a contemporary North Indian folk-song puts it:

The grandfather ran barefoot after the bridal palanquin,
'O father of my son-in-law, please stop for a moment.
Our daughter is going to your house
do not speak to her harshly.
She will plaster your kitchen floor
and clean the pots
but do not send her to fetch water.
She will prepare the bread
and grind the corn
but, please, do not send her to fetch water.
If at the well she smiles at a stranger
both our families will be ruined.'

Western readers will now perhaps be tempted to ask if Indian women are happy. But happiness is mainly a question of expectation and expectation in turn is largely dependent on the models available within a particular culture. Rebellion is not an Indian virtue, equality not an immediate goal. Low caste people and women accept their position as an inevitable result of actions committed in a previous life. Inequality is thus justified since it is ultimately self-imposed and redemption (i.e. actions which will win enough merit to ensure a better re-birth) lies within one's reach. Though unequal, Indian women do not feel inferior to men. By accepting their position as unalterable, they gain self-respect from fulfilling their assigned roles as perfectly as possible. What to a Western woman may look like an unbearable burden of sacrifice, restraint, submission and resignation is to them a positive assertion of their feminine role. Indian women hardly ever wish to be men, nor do they wish to be Western women. Seen from their point of view many of our privileges are horrifying burdens. To be free to choose one's own husband means to expose oneself to the possibility of rejection, humiliation, ridicule and failure – motherhood and marriage are no longer assured. Not to have to submit to one's mother-in-law also means no automatic family support in the bringing-up of one's own children, no daughters-in-law who will take care of one in old age. To choose one's own values instead of simply accepting those prescribed by society means the constant possibility of making the wrong choice and of having to live, unaided, with the consequences. Freedom and security are not always compatible.